Three Ships for Columbus

by Eve Spencer

Alex Haley, General Editor

Illustrations by Tom Sperling

RSVP
RAINTREE STECK-VAUGHN
P U B L I S H E R S
The Steck-Vaughn Company

Austin, Texas

To my mother, with love

Published by Steck-Vaughn Company.

Text, illustrations, and cover art copyright © 1993 by Dialogue Systems, Inc., 627 Broadway, New York, New York 10012. All rights reserved.

Cover art by Tom Sperling

Printed in China

10 788 04

Library of Congress Cataloging-in-Publication Data

Spencer, Eve.
   Three ships for Columbus/by Eve Spencer; illustrations by Tom Sperling.
     p. cm.—(Stories of America)
   Summary: Describes some of the difficulties that Columbus faced on his first voyage to the New World and what he found at the journey's end.
   ISBN 0-8114-7212-4.—ISBN 0-8114-8052-6(pbk.)
   1. Columbus, Christopher—Journeys—America—Juvenile literature. 2. America—Discovery and exploration—Spanish—Juvenile literature. [1. Columbus, Christopher. 2. Explorers. 3. America—Discovery and exploration—Spanish.] I. Sperling, Tom, 1952- ill. II. Title. III. Series.
E118.S64   1993
970.01'5—dc20

92-14401
CIP
AC

ISBN 0–8114–7212–4 (Hardcover)
ISBN 0–8114–8052–6 (Softcover)

A Note
from Alex Haley, General Editor

Many people in North and South America celebrate Columbus Day. Our common history begins in 1492 with Columbus and his three wooden ships. As you will read, his trip was not an easy one.

Our own journey since 1492 has also been hard. Disease and warfare killed millions of American Indians. Slavery, too, left a tragic scar on our history.

But good has also come from the events that followed that October day long ago. We have become Americans. We are a new people, barely 500 years old. We honor courage and freedom. And we are learning to value the rights of all.

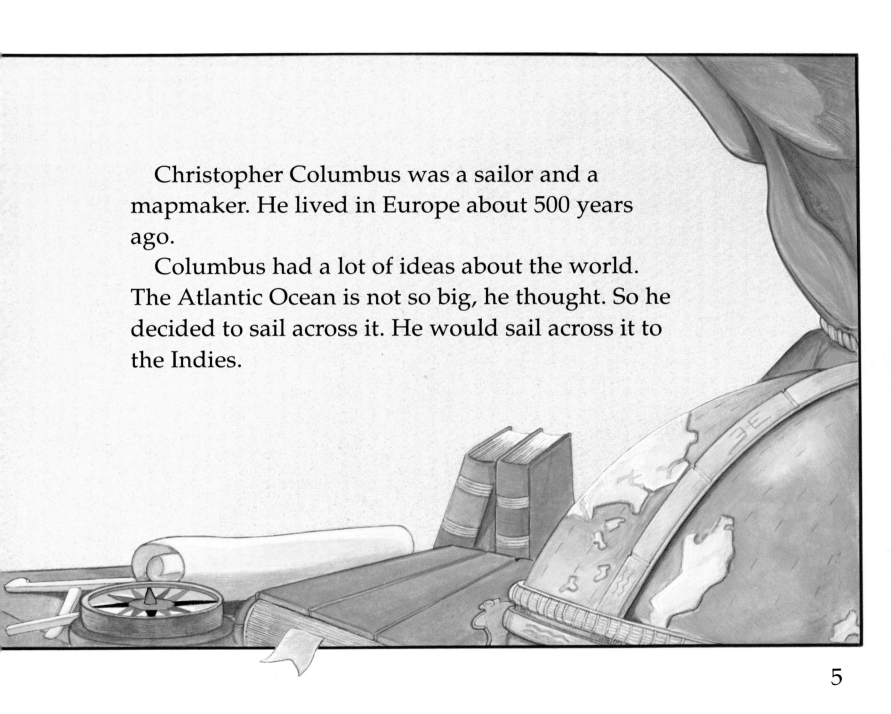

Christopher Columbus was a sailor and a mapmaker. He lived in Europe about 500 years ago.

Columbus had a lot of ideas about the world. The Atlantic Ocean is not so big, he thought. So he decided to sail across it. He would sail across it to the Indies.

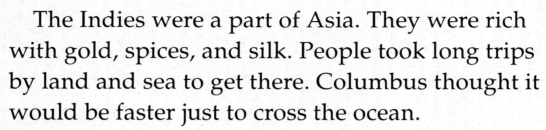

The Indies were a part of Asia. They were rich with gold, spices, and silk. People took long trips by land and sea to get there. Columbus thought it would be faster just to cross the ocean.

Everyone laughed at him. The ocean is too big to cross, they told him. And it is filled with hungry monsters! You will never reach the Indies.

Oh, yes I will, Columbus told them. I will find the fastest way to the Indies.

Columbus asked the King and Queen of Spain to help him with his plan. The King and Queen liked Columbus right away. And they liked the gold Columbus might find. So they agreed to think about his plan.

The King and Queen thought,
and they thought,
and they thought.
They thought about his plan for seven years.
And Columbus waited,
and waited,
and waited.
He waited for an answer for seven years.
Finally, the King and Queen said yes!

The King and Queen gave Columbus three small wooden ships. They were called the *Niña,* the *Pinta,* and the *Santa Maria.* Columbus sailed on the *Santa Maria.* It was the largest of the three ships.

Columbus needed sailors for his ships. But most sailors were afraid to cross the wide, unknown ocean.

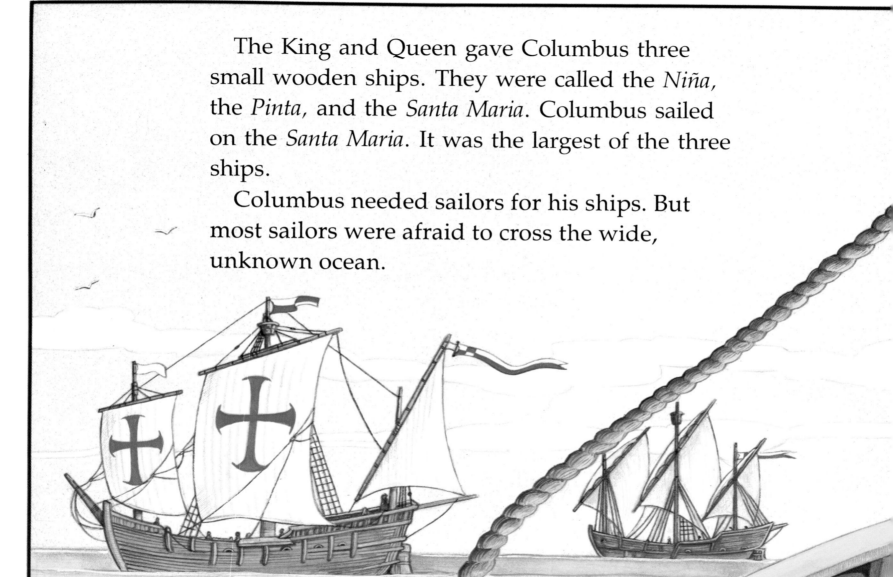

Let someone else go first, they told Columbus.
Not me!
You'll never return!
But finally, ninety sailors said yes.

The ships were very crowded. All of the sailors and all of the supplies had to fit on the three small ships. Columbus had his own cabin. Everyone else had to sleep on the deck.

First Columbus and his ships sailed south to the Canary Islands. Then they were ready to cross the wide ocean.

For one week, the ships sailed west. All went well. Then the ships reached the Sargasso Sea. The Sargasso Sea was full of thick green seaweed. The seaweed closed around the little ships. It grabbed at their sides.

The sailors were very scared. The seaweed will drag us down, they cried. The green sea will swallow us!

Don't worry, Columbus told the sailors. The ships will sail right through the weeds.

And Columbus was right. The ships sailed straight through the Sargasso Sea.

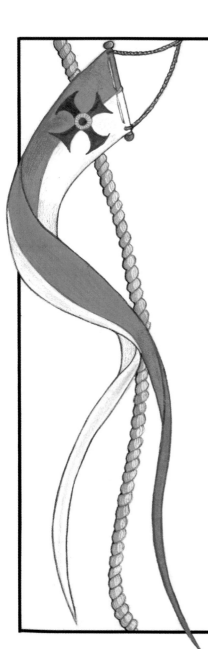

And so the ships sailed on.

They sailed and sailed and sailed.

Every day was the same.

Every day the sailors scrubbed the same decks.

Every day they worked the same sails.

Every day they ate the same thing for breakfast—dry biscuits.

And every day they looked out from the decks and saw the same thing. They saw an endless sky and an endless ocean.

Another week passed. Then another and another. No one had ever sailed this long without seeing land. When would the ocean end?

The sailors were scared. Four weeks is too long to sail, they said. Take us back to Spain, Columbus! Take us back or we will throw you overboard!

Calm down! Columbus ordered. Think of the gold we will find. Think of the silks and spices. We will be rich, he said.

And I know we are near land. I will make a promise. We will turn back if we do not find land in three days.

Then Columbus ordered the ships to sail not just all day, but all night too! The night wind filled the sails, and the ships sailed on through the darkness. Would it be enough?

Columbus was lucky. On October 12, just two days later, a sailor spotted an island.

"Land!" he yelled out. "Land!"

Columbus and his sailors shouted for joy. They sang songs and thanked God for bringing them safely to the Indies.

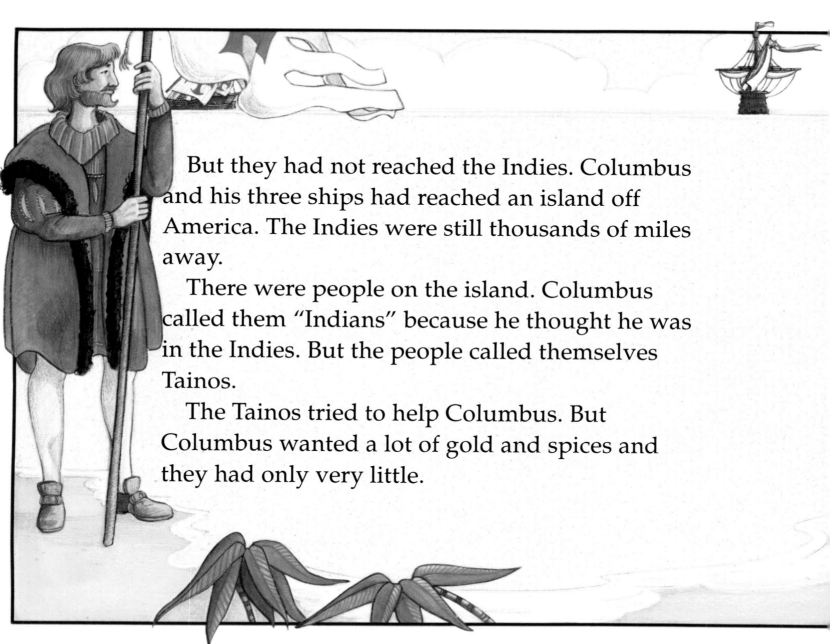

But they had not reached the Indies. Columbus and his three ships had reached an island off America. The Indies were still thousands of miles away.

There were people on the island. Columbus called them "Indians" because he thought he was in the Indies. But the people called themselves Tainos.

The Tainos tried to help Columbus. But Columbus wanted a lot of gold and spices and they had only very little.

So Columbus and his men left the island. And for three months they sailed the waters of the Caribbean Sea. They sailed from island...to island...to island.

They found foods they had never seen before—tomatoes, pumpkins, and corn. But where were the great cities of the Indies? Where were the riches they were seeking? Not here.

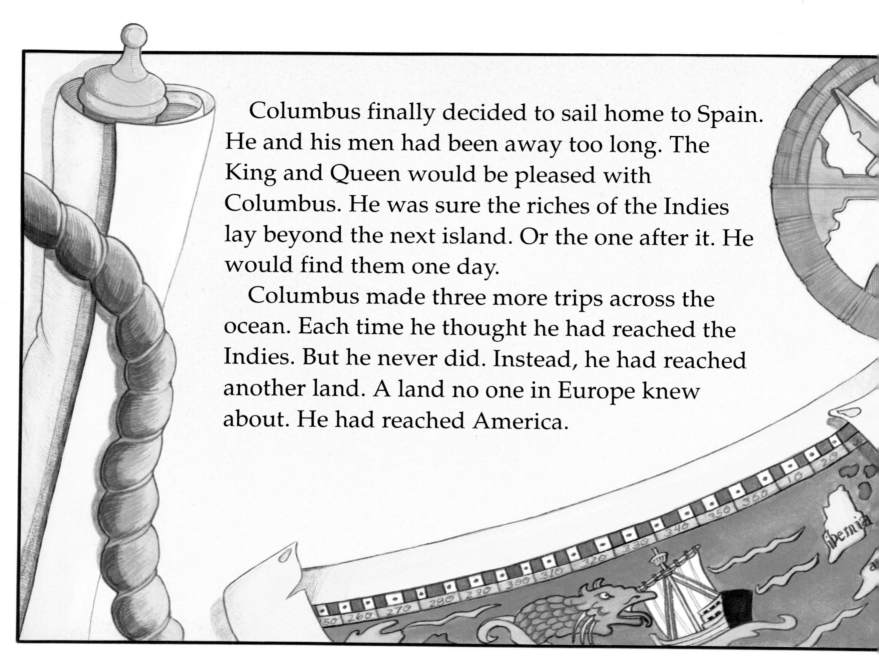

Columbus finally decided to sail home to Spain. He and his men had been away too long. The King and Queen would be pleased with Columbus. He was sure the riches of the Indies lay beyond the next island. Or the one after it. He would find them one day.

Columbus made three more trips across the ocean. Each time he thought he had reached the Indies. But he never did. Instead, he had reached another land. A land no one in Europe knew about. He had reached America.

After Columbus, people came from every land and for every reason. And they're still coming today. But it began with Columbus, his three ships, and the cry of "Land!" on October 12, 1492.

Columbus Day

Columbus Day is celebrated in cities and towns all across the Americas. On this day, people honor Columbus's famous voyage of 1492.

There are parades with marching bands, banners, and flags. It is an important holiday to many people.

In the United States, Columbus Day is celebrated on the second Monday in October. Many schools and businesses are closed. In our country Columbus day is especially important to Italian Americans. They are proud that Columbus came from Italy. Spanish Americans are proud, too, because Columbus made his journey for Spain.